Creative Lives

JANE AUSTEN

Kristen Rajczak Nelson

CREATED BY Humans

Published in 2026 by The Rosen Publishing Group, Inc.
2544 Clinton Street, Buffalo, NY 14224

Editor: Kristen Nelson
Designer: Michael Flynn

Photo Credits: Cover, p. 5 https://en.wikipedia.org/wiki/Jane_Austen; (series background) Yuliya Chsherbakova/Shutterstock.com; p. 7 https://commons.wikimedia.org/wiki/File:RicePortrait.jpg; p. 9 Dmitry Naumov/Shutterstock.com; p. 11 https://commons.wikimedia.org/wiki/File:Austen_-_Juvenilia_(Volume_1).pdf; p. 13 https://commons.wikimedia.org/wiki/File:Lady_Susan_Manuscript_103.png; p. 15 https://en.wikipedia.org/wiki/File:Pickering_-_Greatbatch_-_Jane_Austen_-_Pride_and_Prejudice_-_She_then_told_him_what_Mr._Darcy_had_voluntarily_done_for_Lydia.jpg; p. 17 Claudia Longo/Shutterstock.com; p. 19 Akhmad Dody Firmansyah/Shutterstock.com; p. 21 https://commons.wikimedia.org/wiki/File:Grave_of_Jane_Austen_in_Winchester_Cathedral_(5204818136).jpg.

Cataloging-in-Publication Data
Names: Rajczak Nelson, Kristen.
Title: Jane Austen / Kristen Rajczak Nelson.
Description: Buffalo, NY : Created by Humans, an imprint of Rosen Publishing, 2026. | Series: Creative lives | Includes glossary and index.
Identifiers: ISBN 9781534552456 (pbk.) | ISBN 9781534552463 (library bound) | ISBN 9781534552470 (ebook)
Subjects: LCSH: Austen, Jane, 1775-1817--Juvenile literature. | Novelists, English--19th century--Biography--Juvenile literature.
Classification: LCC PR4036.R354 2026 | DDC 823.7--dc23

Manufactured in the United States of America

CPSIA Compliance Information: Batch #CWCBH26. For Further Information contact Rosen Publishing at 1-800-237-9932.

CONTENTS

Writer of Her Time

Jane Austen wrote her best-known **novels** more than 200 years ago. Austen looked at the world around her and used what she saw to **create** timeless stories and characters. She led a creative life, though she didn't live to be very old.

Early Life

Austen was born in southeast England on December 16, 1775. She lived with her parents, six brothers, and one sister. Her father, George, was a **rector**. He also ran a school for local boys. Austen's mother, Cassandra, kept the family home.

Austen didn't go to school. She was taught at home. Austen had **access** to a large library because of the school her father ran in their home. Growing up, Austen was very close with her sister, also named Cassandra.

Child Writer

Austen began writing as a child. She wrote funny stories, plays, short stories, and more. Some of this writing has **survived** to present day. It's sometimes called the Austen's **juvenilia**. These **manuscripts** were written from about 1787 to 1793.

Volume the First

When Austen was around 19, she finished a novella, or short novel. It was called *Lady Susan*. The novella was made up of letters. It wasn't published, or put out as a book, until after Austen died.

rightly understanding each other's meaning. — This idea struck me at the moment, & I instantly determined that an accidental dispute in which I might probably be as much to blame as himself, should not deprive you of your Brother. — If you remember, I left the room almost immediately. — I was resolved to lose no time in clearing up these mistakes as far as I could. — The case was this. — Frederica had set herself violently against marrying Sir James —"

— "And can your Ladyship wonder that she should?" cried I with some warmth. — Frederica has an excellent understanding, & Sir James has none."

"I am at least very far from regretting it, my dear Sister, said she; on the contrary, I am grateful for so favourable a sign of my Daughter's sense. Sir James is certainly under par — (his boyish manners make him appear the worse) — & had Frederica possessed the penetration, the abilities, which

From Life

Austen started writing some of her famous novels in her early 20s. She wrote about people living their everyday lives in England during the late 1700s and early 1800s. Austen used her own life, family, and friends as **inspiration**.

Known For

Austen began work on her most well-known novels, *Sense and Sensibility* and *Pride and Prejudice*, in the late 1790s. Her family moved around a lot in the early 1800s. Her father died in 1805. However, the following years were busy with writing these and other novels.

WORDSWORTH CLASSICS
JANE AUSTEN
Sense and Sensibility
COMPLETE AND UNABRIDGED

Sense and Sensibility came out in 1811. It was published anonymously, which means it didn't have Austen's name on it. Between 1813 and 1815, three more of her novels were published: *Pride and Prejudice, Mansfield Park,* and *Emma*.

Pride and Prejudice
Jane Austen
Emma
Jane Austen
Mansfield Park
Jane Austen

Early Death

Austen became sick and died in July 1817. Soon after her death, her family published two more of her novels. Austen's brother also announced her as the author of all her work after she died. Her grave at Winchester Cathedral is visited by many honoring her creative life.

In Memory of
JANE AUSTEN,
youngeſt daughter of the late
Revd GEORGE AUSTEN,
formerly Rector of Steventon in this County
ſhe departed this Life on the 18th of July 1817,
aged 41, after a long illneſs ſupported with
the patience and the hopes of a Chriſtian.
The benevolence of her heart,
the ſweetneſs of her temper, and
the extraordinary endowments of her mind
obtained the regard of all who knew her and
the warmeſt love of her intimate connections.
Their grief is in proportion to their affection
they know their loſs to be irreparable,
but in their deepeſt affliction they are conſoled
by a firm though humble hope that her charity,
devotion, faith and purity, have rendered
her ſoul acceptable in the ſight of her
REDEEMER.

GLOSSARY

access: The ability to enter.

create: To make using one's imagination.

inspiration: Something that causes someone to want to make something.

juvenilia: Works of art created during an artist's youth.

manuscript: Handwritten piece of writing.

novel: A book that tells a story.

rector: A leader in charge of a faith group.

survive: To exist.

FOR MORE INFORMATION

BOOKS

Camlin, Anne, and Jane Austen. *Mismatched: A Modern Graphic Retelling of Emma*. New York, NY: Little, Brown and Company, 2024.

Favilli, Elena, and Francesca Cavallo. *Good Night Stories for Rebel Girls: More Than 100 Tales of Extraordinary Women.* Santa Monica, CA: Rebel Girls, 2025.

WEBSITES

Jane Austen
www.janeausten.org
Learn more about Austen's life and work,

Jane Austen Society of North America
jasna.org
Find out information about Austen here.

Publisher's note to educators and parents: Our editors have carefully reviewed these websites to ensure that they are suitable for students. Many websites change frequently, however, and we cannot guarantee that a site's future contents will continue to meet our high standards of quality and educational value. Be advised that students should be closely supervised whenever they access the internet.

INDEX